IMAGES
of America

A HISTORY OF ALCATRAZ ISLAND SINCE 1853

IMAGES
of America

A HISTORY OF
ALCATRAZ ISLAND
SINCE 1853

Gregory L. Wellman

ARCADIA
PUBLISHING

Published by Arcadia Publishing
Charleston, South Carolina

Printed in the United States of America

Library of Congress Catalog Card Number: 2022932950

For all general information contact Arcadia Publishing at:
Telephone 843-853-2070
Fax 843-853-0044
E-mail sales@arcadiapublishing.com
For customer service and orders:
Toll-Free 1-888-313-2665

Visit us on the Internet at www.arcadiapublishing.com

*To my mother, Deborah; my sister Gabrielle;
and the memory of my father, Frank Wellman.*

CONTENTS

ACKNOWLEDGMENTS

My deepest gratitude goes to Chuck Stucker, a member of the Alcatraz Alumni Association, for photographs, time, interviews, and a plethora of information. Without his help and the help of the Alcatraz Alumni Association, this book would have been near impossible. If you have worked or lived on Alcatraz, please visit their website at www.alcatrazalumni.org.

A special thank-you is given to everyone on the Arcadia Publishing team. Thanks go to my friend and colleague Martha Blakney for her advice, proofreading, and research assistance. A thank-you is owed to Amanda Williford at the Golden Gate National Archives for retrieving, providing, and helping me to establish licensing for many of the photographs under tight timelines. To all my mentors who have helped me become a better historian, especially David Rubiales for introducing California history to me, Dr. Sally Harvey, Dr. Aaron Cohen, and Dr. Christopher Castaneda, thank you. Many thanks go to Alcatraz historian John Martini for his research, publications, and help. I appreciate Alcatraz historian Michael Esslinger for his advice concerning photographs and historical details. Special thanks are due to my family and friends who have supported me throughout my work on these various editions.

The history of Alcatraz is vast, and I have tried to cover the essential portions of the island's history. It is impossible to mention every guard, prisoner, and family member who has lived on the island. This book profiles only a handful of them. I hope this does justice to the legacy of Alcatraz.

INTRODUCTION

Alcatraz, a sandstone island in the San Francisco Bay, gained its place in American history as one of the most notorious prisons in the United States. Some of America's most infamous criminals were sent to serve out their prison sentences on Alcatraz. Men like Al Capone and Machine Gun Kelly spent a portion of their lives on the island. Criminals of this stature and its sheer inescapability made Alcatraz one of the most infamous prisons in American history. Today, it has become one of San Francisco's most popular tourist attractions after opening to the public in the 1970s as part of the Golden Gate National Recreation Area. Alcatraz has been a setting in American pop culture, in movies, video games, and many books. The island's role in American history dates to the late 1840s with the origins of the Bear Republic of California, and its history prior to that is as old as the bay itself.

The history of Alcatraz before European discovery is mostly undocumented. The first people to occupy the area now known as the San Francisco Bay were Native American tribes of the Ohlone and Coastal Miwok. How long they occupied the Bay Area is unclear; estimates gauge their presence around the bay for thousands of years before European discovery. The Ohlone and Coastal Miwok flourished in the San Francisco Bay for centuries, until the Spanish invasion of California in the 18th century. By the early to mid-18th century, the Spanish crown was exploring more of the region, making settlements further into the heart of California. Reports of Russian fur trappers coming from the north toward Monterey accelerated Spanish settlement in the region. These reports led to new Spanish expeditions north, and the eventual discovery of the San Francisco Bay.

The Spanish discovery of the bay and the first documentation of the island that would become known as Alcatraz was by a band of soldiers led by Capt. Gaspar de Portola, who overshot their original destination of Monterey and happened upon the bay in 1769. At the time, the large body of water was believed to be landlocked until the discovery of the Golden Gate by Capt. Pedro Fages, who found the peninsula gap in 1770. Five years later, the *San Carlos*, commanded by Lt. Juan Manuel de Ayala, was the first recorded Spanish ship to explore the bay. Upon charting its islands, Ayala discovered one covered with a large number of pelicans; this island would become known as La Isla de los Alcatraces, or "island of pelicans" or "island of large birds." This name eventually evolved into Alcatraz.

For the next 46 years, Spain remained in control of California and the San Francisco Bay until Mexican independence in 1821. Six years after Mexican independence, a more accurate chart was made of the bay. In 1827, when Capt. Fredrick Beechey of the British Royal Navy was allowed to explore the bay, his more detailed map cemented the name La Isla de los Alcatraces, or Alcatraz Island. Later examination of Ayala's original charts shows that the name "de los Alcatraces" was actually placed on Yerba Buena Island, and it was not until Beechey's more extensive examination of the bay and his rearrangement of the islands' names that Alcatraz officially received its name.

After the Mexican–American War in 1848, the United States gained a huge portion of land from the Mexican government. This included California, the San Francisco Bay, and the island known as Alcatraces. The US Coast Guard finally decided upon the name Alcatraz in 1851. The island at the time was still a barren rock covered with pelicans, but this soon changed as the US military developed plans for an outpost on the island. By 1853, the United States was developing the island as a fort designed to protect San Francisco Bay. Military development continued throughout the 19th century and into the first two decades of the 20th century. As the fort expanded, its functions changed. By the late 19th century, with the rise of the Spanish-American War, the prison population grew drastically, resulting in new, more elaborate prisons and barracks. By 1915, the fort was no longer considered an effective military defense post, and the fort was used only as a military prison from that point forward. There was also a designation change. Alcatraz was now designated as Pacific Branch, US Disciplinary Barracks. The military prison lasted another 17 years until 1933, when the fate of Alcatraz changed and prison authority moved from military to federal jurisdiction under the US Federal Bureau of Prisons.

As a federal prison, Alcatraz gained a reputation as a place for only the most incorrigible prisoners. The prisoners sentenced to do time there, the high-profile crimes they committed, and the desolation that Alcatraz left them with as a punishment made the island notorious in the minds of the American population. The term "The Rock" was born during the 1940s. The name came from soldiers who served on Alcatraz as part of an antiaircraft post during World War II. Over the years, the island saw its share of attempted escapes, riots, and other exploits that raised its level of fame higher and higher. The federal penitentiary survived until 1963, when the prisoners were moved to new locations, and the guards and their families were sent to new duties and new homes. Alcatraz penitentiary officially closed for good.

Following its closure, Alcatraz sat stagnant for six years until 1969, when, for 19 months, Native Americans from a variety of tribes claimed the island for themselves in what was known as the Native American Occupation of Alcatraz. Following a peaceful ending to the occupation in 1971, Congress added Alcatraz to the Golden Gate Recreational Area in 1972. Alcatraz since then has become one of America's most famous prisons and landmarks. Throughout its history, the island's development and changes reflect the political, social, and economic changes occurring in the United States.

One

A NEW PURPOSE FOR ALCATRAZ

THE CALIFORNIA GOLD RUSH, THE MILITARY, AND THE 19TH CENTURY

James Marshall discovered gold in Coloma, California, on January 24, 1848, changing the development and settlement of the territory drastically. Nine days later on February 2, 1848, the Mexican–American War was settled through the Treaty of Guadalupe Hidalgo. The treaty granted the United States 525,000 square miles of northwestern Mexican territory, including California. Two years later in 1850, California gained statehood, bringing with it the small island in the San Francisco Bay, Alcatraz. The Gold Rush marked a vast demographic change with the influx of hundreds of thousands of people setting out to find their fortune in the West. It also marked a change for California as it became more strategically and economically important to the federal government; millions of dollars' worth of gold was mined from California goldfields. These economic and demographic growths created a greater need for the defense of California by the US military. The need to secure the bay was imperative as it became an essential point of defense for Northern California.

Alcatraz, along with other strategic points, were chosen to become the frontline of defense in case of an attack on California via San Francisco Bay. By 1853, construction of the military installation on the island had begun. Alcatraz would stand as one of the main lines of defense against ships coming through the Golden Gate. That same year, the first lighthouse in California was constructed on the island. Alcatraz simultaneously functioned as a fortress and a military prison. For 80 years, it held some of the worst military prisoners—Confederate conspirators during the Civil War and military deserters during the Spanish-American War. Alcatraz continued as a fortress until 1907, when the island was deemed obsolete as a defensive position, becoming simply a prison for the Western military. This lasted until 1933, when administration of the island was transferred to the Federal Bureau of Prisons.

Pictured in 1853, Alcatraz Island is the small island at left between Angel Island in the background and San Francisco proper in the foreground. This view from Nob Hill shows Alcatraz before any major developments. Two years before this photograph, the Army authorized construction of a fortress there to protect the bay. The newly formed Board of Engineers of the Pacific Coast oversaw construction of forts on Alcatraz, Lime Point, and Fort Point. (Courtesy of Chuck Stucker.)

Zealous Bates Tower was put in charge of construction of the fort. Due to the isolation of California during the 1850s, communicating and getting military supplies and building materials took several months, which delayed the construction of the fort. Construction was also delayed by skyrocketing costs and desertion of workers to pursue mining opportunities in the goldfields. (Courtesy of the Aztec Club of 1847, www.aztecclub.com.)

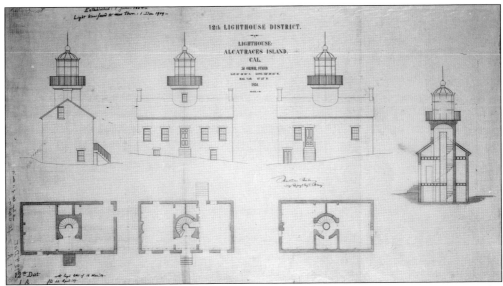

Aside from a military fort, Alcatraz was home to the first lighthouse on the West Coast. The growth of California's and San Francisco's populations brought many ships into the bay, and the need for a lighthouse grew exponentially. These blueprints from 1854 show the design for the new lighthouse in the Cape Cod cottage style. (US Coast Guard. Courtesy of Golden Gate NRA Park Archives, PAM Negative Collection, GOGA 35256.0541.)

The lighthouse construction was completed in 1853. The lens that powered the lighthouse was imported from France. It arrived in New York and was promptly shipped around South America to San Francisco. It was lit on June 1, 1854, and would continue to illuminate the bay for another 62 years. This photograph shows the lighthouse in 1854 after the military fort was established. (Courtesy of Chuck Stucker.)

In 1857, the military decided that Alcatraz would need a citadel. By 1859, the citadel was complete; it remained on the island for the next 49 years, until 1908. The citadel's purpose changed over the years. It was designed as a last point of military defense, and the structure consisted of a basement that was surrounded by a dry moat and two aboveground levels. The basement was used to house the kitchen, bakery, bedrooms, storerooms, and individual jail cells. The top levels were used as military personnel quarters, servant quarters, parlors, and a mess room. The large cylinders on the roof were water tanks used to hold fresh water for the island. In 1882, the citadel was converted into larger living quarters for officers and their families to use during their tour of duty on Alcatraz. Eventually, the citadel was torn down to make way for the third prison in 1908. (Courtesy of Chuck Stucker.)

Maj. Gen. James Birdseye McPherson is seen here on a $2 bond. Known for his valor during the Civil War, McPherson became one of most famous soldiers to serve on Alcatraz Island. He was transferred to Alcatraz early in his career in 1858, taking command of construction on the island's defenses. In 1859, McPherson relinquished his command to Capt. Joseph Stewart and transferred from the island in 1861 at the beginning of the Civil War. After returning to New York, he quickly moved up the ranks of the Union Army, reaching major general one year later in 1862. Fighting under General Sherman, he later gained command of the Tennessee Army. McPherson was killed later that year in Georgia. He became one of the most revered soldiers of the Civil War. (Courtesy of the Federal Reserve Bank of San Francisco.)

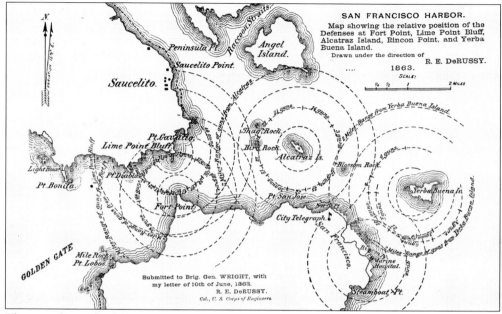

This map shows the different defensive positions in San Francisco Bay during the Civil War. The rings represent the cannon range of each fort. Of the five defensive positions, Alcatraz was in the center, behind Lime Point and Fort Point at the entrance of the bay. (Courtesy of the Golden Gate NRA Park Archives, Fort Point Collection, GOGA 2042.)

Alcatraz's use as a military penitentiary grew during the Civil War as more men were arrested for treason. Alcatraz had been used by the military to hold prisoners since 1859, although by 1863, it needed a new formal prison. This photograph shows the 1863 lower prison cells that were constructed for this purpose. These cells were incredibly small and a fire hazard—inhumane by today's standards. (Courtesy of Chuck Stucker.)

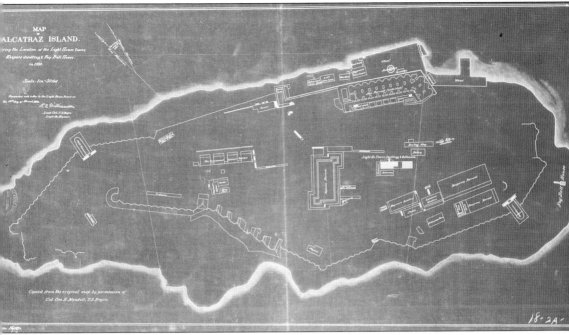

This 1880 map shows the layout of the military structures on Alcatraz. At left is the northwest tip of Alcatraz, where the Battery of Rosecranz and Halleck are positioned. The large building at the top right (east) corner of the island is the barracks. The south Battery of McClellan is just above the south point Fog Bell House. At the bottom is the western Battery of McPherson, connecting with the northwestern Batteries of Stevens and Mansfield. In the left center of the island are the parade grounds. The citadel is the large building to the right, followed by the smaller rectangle to the right, which represents the lighthouse. Finally, the larger rectangles just below the lighthouse are temporary barracks. (Courtesy of the Golden Gate NRA Park Archives, TASC Negative Collection, GOGA 35301.1985.)

In this photograph of south Battery McClellan in 1868, the cannon in the background is a 15-inch Rodman gun. These guns were capable of firing a 330-pound explosive shot 4,680 yards when angled at a 25-degree elevation. Weighing over 25 tons, these were the largest guns mounted on the island. (Courtesy of Chuck Stucker.)

The lithograph shows Alcatraz in the early 1870s. As new technologies emerged following the Civil War, the defenses of Alcatraz were becoming outdated and ineffective against modern warships. The only weapons that were a match for the new ironclad ships were the 15-inch Rodman guns. This forced the Army to redesign Alcatraz. (Courtesy of Chuck Stucker.)

Some enlisted men and an officer stand on the Alcatraz dock. This photograph shows the military uniforms of the period—standard issue was blue. The officer wears white gloves with his dress uniform. (Courtesy of Chuck Stucker.)

Prisoners did much of the labor that changed the layout of the island over the 80 years of military jurisdiction. In the 1870s, under Maj. George Mendell's planning, prisoner labor reduced Alcatraz's natural peaks and created a level top area on the island. Their labor also increased the actual size of the island when they dumped the excess dirt and rock into the bay, filling coves and changing the natural landscape drastically. This photograph shows prisoners reducing a hill on the north end of the island. (Courtesy of Chuck Stucker.)

Prisoners were not the only means of labor; animals were also used to transport large goods around the island. Here, two mules pull a wagon in front of the finance office. Mules were used because they were more efficient than horses on the steep switchbacks of Alcatraz. (Courtesy of Chuck Stucker.)

Throughout the 1880s, the island evolved, and by the 1890s, it had transformed drastically. Bustling with military personnel and a growing prison population, the island was essentially a small city in the bay. This picture shows the influence of Victorian architecture on the island as more structures were created. During the late 1890s, the Alcatraz population skyrocketed because of the Spanish-American War, creating a need for more modern structures. Note the bombproof barracks next to the dock. These were later transformed into Building No. 64. (Courtesy of Chuck Stucker.)

One of the main ways to get to Alcatraz was aboard military transport ships. The *General McPherson*, named after Gen. George McPherson, was used to transport a variety of supplies to the island as well as prisoners and soldiers. Here, the *McPherson* is docked at Alcatraz, carrying a large number of soldiers. (Courtesy of Chuck Stucker.)

The main entrance to the island must have struck newcomers with great intimidation. This was the view seen by anyone coming from the dock to the first prison. There was a long, dreary corridor known as the sally port below the first prison library that anyone entering the island had to walk through to get to the main grounds. (National Archives RG 92. Courtesy of Golden Gate NRA Park Archives, Interpretation Negative Collection, GOGA 2316.)

Once through the sally port and on Alcatraz, the island appeared like a small city. By the 1890s, the island needed modern necessities, one of which was a fully functional hospital, constructed during the late 19th century. The hospital is seen here in 1893. Five years later, the hospital was essential in providing medical care for the growing military and prison population during the Spanish-American War. (Courtesy of Chuck Stucker.)

Officers lived well on Alcatraz. This wooden walkway once led to officers' row, and the buildings represent the Victorian style of that era. The development of the island over the past 40 years had been drastic, and these buildings were one aspect of that growth. (Courtesy of Chuck Stucker.)

During the 1890s, nineteen Hopi men were sent to Alcatraz, some of the last Native Americans to be imprisoned on the island. The US military arrested them in 1894 after a conflict in the Arizona territory, and they were transferred to Alcatraz in January 1895 from Fort Defiance. Their imprisonment at Alcatraz lasted until August 1895. From 1873 to 1895, a total of 32 Native Americans from various tribes were imprisoned on Alcatraz. (Courtesy of Chuck Stucker.)

At the turn of the 20th century, the second "upper" prison of the island was built. Seen here in 1902, this prison was later expanded in 1904 to replace the outdated lower prison altogether. The renovated prison held 307 inmates and was equipped with new amenities for the prisoners. This upper prison was the main hold on Alcatraz until the new concrete prison was created eight years later in 1912. (Courtesy of Chuck Stucker.)

Seen here in 1903, inmates line up front to back to be counted. This type of head count made sure there were no escapes. (Courtesy of the Golden Gate NRA Park Archives, Interpretation Negative Collection, GOGA 2316.)

Positioned at the north end of Alcatraz was the fog bell that warned approaching ships of the island's location. Note the size of the bell just to the left of the soldier in the opening of the house. It could be heard for miles, alerting ships coming into the bay. (Courtesy of the Golden Gate NRA Park Archives, Interpretation Negative Collection, GOGA 2316.)

At approximately 5:12 a.m. on April 18, 1906, one of the greatest catastrophes in San Francisco history occurred. An earthquake followed by a fire destroyed most of the city. Due to the fire, city jailers were forced to move their prisoners from the mainland to Alcatraz, where they would remain for nine days. The earthquake had little effect on Alcatraz, leaving only minor damage and making it an ideal layover for the prisoners. This 1906 photograph shows just how devastating the blaze was, consuming many of the buildings in San Francisco. It would take years for the city to recover from the devastation. (Courtesy of the Golden Gate NRA Park Archives, Letterman Army Medical Center Photo File, GOGA 35288.195.)

The year 1907 marked a pivotal change for Alcatraz. The island would no longer be used by the military as a point of defense for San Francisco Bay. Alcatraz was now designated US Military Prison, Alcatraz Island, and official military prison guards replaced the infantrymen who once guarded the inmates. During the same year, Col. Rueben Turner was appointed commandant of Alcatraz (until 1911) and was given the task of designing the third prison—the legendary building that still stands on the island today. With a $250,000 budget, Turner was ordered to design a new "state-of-the-art prison," according to John Martini in *Fortress Alcatraz: Guardian of the Golden Gate*. The prison would be made of concrete and have electricity and steam heaters. (Courtesy of the Golden Gate NRA Park Archives, Col. Ruben Turner Collection, GOGA 3078.)

Construction of Turner's prison began in 1910. Like many of the other structures on Alcatraz, this prison would also be constructed using prisoner labor. Preparation took several years, but construction was completed in only two. (National Archives RG92. Courtesy of the Golden Gate NRA Park Archives, Interpretation Negative Collection, GOGA 2316.)

Seen here in 1909, the ironwork of the new prison was higher than the dome on the original lighthouse. This marked the end of California's first lighthouse. It was torn down and replaced with the second lighthouse, which still serves as a beacon for the bay today. (National Archives RG92. Courtesy of the Golden Gate NRA Park Archives, Interpretation Negative Collection, GOGA 2316.)

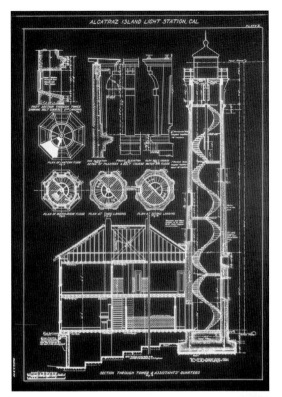

These schematics of the new lighthouse show that the modern concrete design was far superior to the cottage style of the first lighthouse. The base of the lighthouse was designed to house up to three lighthouse keepers and their families. The keepers maintained the light atop the new 84-foot tower as well as the fog bells on the island. Lighthouse keepers remained on the island for 54 years, until 1963, when they were replaced by an automated beacon system. (Left, US Coast Guard. Courtesy of the Golden Gate NRA Park Archives, TASC Negative Collection, GOGA 35301.0824. Below, US Coast Guard. Courtesy of the Golden Gate NRA Park Archives, TASC Negative Collection, GOGA 35301.0826.)

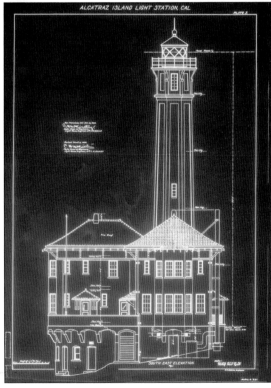

In 1970, a fire set by Native American occupiers destroyed the lighthouse keepers' quarters. Although it was not rebuilt, the tower of the lighthouse still stands and shines light upon the bay. (Courtesy of Chuck Stucker.)

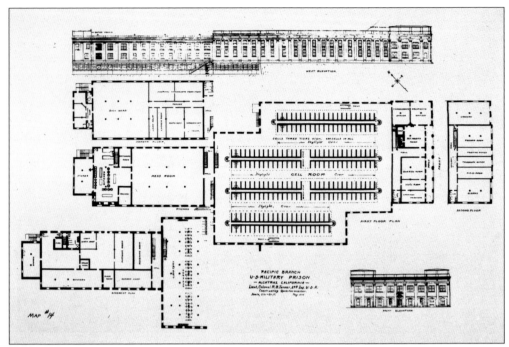

Above is Turner's original layout for the prison. The 1909 map below shows the new layout for the island. (Above, National Archives. Courtesy of the Golden Gate NRA Park Archives, Interpretation Negative Collection, GOGA 2316. Below, courtesy Chuck Stucker's private collection.)

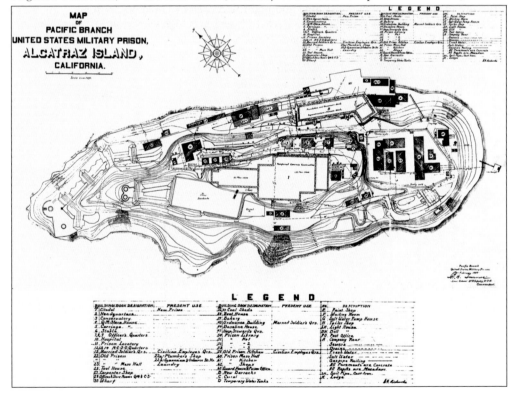

In 1912, the new prison was complete. Considered an engineering feat for the time, it was, according to Michael Esslinger's *Alcatraz: A Definitive History of the Penitentiary Years*, "the largest concrete structure in the world" at 500 feet long and had the capacity to hold 600 prisoners. The cells, designed to hold only one prisoner, were stacked three levels high with four different cellblocks labeled A, B, C, and D. (Courtesy of Chuck Stucker.)

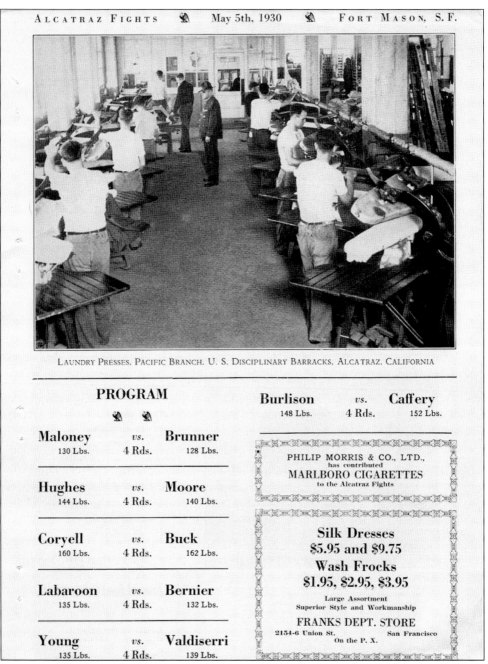

The early 20th century brought a new dynamic to Alcatraz with Friday night fights, sanctioned boxing matches between inmates arranged by the military. Invited civilians and soldiers from posts around the Bay Area would come to Alcatraz to watch these bouts. At the end of the night, there was a "battle royal," consisting of multiple blindfolded boxers fighting all at once. Pictured here is a flyer for the match on May 5, 1930. It includes a photograph of the prisoners working in the laundry facilities on Alcatraz, the matchups, and two small advertisements—one for Phillip Morris and Company, which contributed Marlboro cigarettes to the fights, and Franks Department Store, which was selling silk dresses for $5.95 and $9.75. (Courtesy of Chuck Stucker.)

Two

ALCATRAZ EVOLVES UNDER THE FEDERAL BUREAU OF PRISONS

1933–1963

In 1933, Alcatraz's jurisdiction was transferred from the military to the Federal Bureau of Prisons. The transfer was a result of a number of factors. Throughout the 19th century, the military had received bad publicity for operating a prison in the middle of San Francisco Bay. Prone to the occasional escape attempt, Alcatraz was covered regularly by the press. Along with the ever-growing upkeep costs, Alcatraz was becoming a burden for the military. The Federal Bureau of Prisons' interest in Alcatraz was a result of the growth of the US prison population and ineffective prisons throughout the country during the 1920s and early 1930s. Enforcement of Prohibition during the Roaring Twenties heavily impacted the US prison system, with growth in the prison population from convictions of mobsters and bootleggers. With this rise, the Federal Bureau of Prisons needed more elaborate prisons. The concept of a new maximum-security prison was introduced to thwart escapes and hold the worst of the worst of America's inmate population. Alcatraz would provide the perfect site for the bureau's new prison experiment.

The agreement to transfer Alcatraz to federal jurisdiction was completed on October 13, 1933. Alcatraz underwent an extensive $260,000 overhaul to make it suitable for use as a maximum-security penitentiary. New steel bars were installed throughout much of the prison to replace outdated strap steel bars, and cell doors began using an automated locking system to help prevent escapes. Aside from reinforced security within the prison, there were also additional structures built throughout the island to prevent escapes. New gates were installed to secure different areas, and six different guard towers were constructed.

After the security changes, the Federal Bureau of Prisons implemented many other structural changes. Some of the old military buildings were renovated or removed. New technologies were implemented, and a variety of ships were used to move water, food, people, and other supplies to the island. This chapter will elaborate on the changes on the island over the 30 years of Federal Bureau of Prisons control along with what the interior of the prison facilities once looked like.

Alcatraz is one and a half miles from the San Francisco docks. Signs posted all around the island reminded everyone that only government ships were allowed on Alcatraz and that civilian ships had to remain at least 200 yards offshore. No one was allowed ashore without a pass. (Courtesy of Chuck Stucker.)

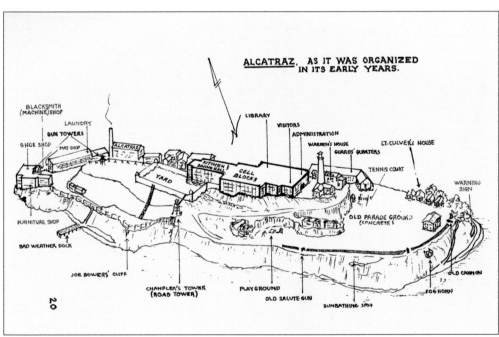

Once a child living on Alcatraz, Roy "Rocky" Chandler, son of guard E.F. Chandler, drew the different areas and their functions in this map. It shows the location of the new guard towers and various other buildings. Chandler also described other aspects of the island, like the sunbathing spot at lower left and the tennis courts to the right just below the lighthouse, both on the old military parade grounds. (Courtesy of Chuck Stucker.)

To enter the cellblocks on Alcatraz, one would have to come and go through this door. It was about four inches thick, seven feet tall, and five feet wide. Made of solid steel, it made escaping through the front door almost impossible without the key. (Courtesy of Chuck Stucker.)

A Chip of The old "ROCK" ALCATRAZ

To get through the cellblock door, or any other door in the prison, this was the key to have. It was used to open most locks throughout the prison. (Courtesy of Chuck Stucker.)

Clockwise from top left are A block, B block (also known as Broadway), D block (which led to the library), a standard five-foot-by-nine-foot prisoner's cell, and a solitary confinement cell, which were located at the end of D block. Solitary cells were almost pitch-black inside. (Courtesy of Chuck Stucker.)

This was the prison library, which could be entered through a door at the end of cellblock D. Like every other activity on the island, the library was a privilege for prisoners. It consisted of 15,000 books and magazines. The average prisoner read about 75 to 100 books a year, and the National Parks Service claimed that the prisoners "read more serious literature than does an ordinary person in the community." (Courtesy of Chuck Stucker.)

The floors shine from a fresh buff in the prisoners' mess hall. On August 12, 1954, the menu consisted of beef barbecue, natural gravy, mashed potatoes, buttered carrots and peas, tossed salad, peach upside down cake, bread, and coffee. Dinner was at 4:40 p.m. sharp. (Courtesy of Chuck Stucker.)

Here is the left side of the kitchen where prisoners on mess duty would prepare meals for the whole island, including the guards and prison staff. At times, this could be a dangerous place because prisoners had access to knives for cooking. (Courtesy of Chuck Stucker.)

Pictured here are the original dining tables used by the prisoners. Each table had bench-style seats that could hold up to six men per side. The tables and chairs later changed to a style that held only four men. The presumption has been made that these smaller tables allowed prisoners to talk among themselves and conspire to escape. During breakfast, lunch, and dinner, the entire prisoner population ate together, filling the mess hall. The guards working the dining area were drastically outnumbered, making the risk of attack even greater. The officers' only backup were the tear gas canisters attached to the ceiling. These canisters gave the mess hall its nickname: "the gas chamber." (Both, courtesy of Chuck Stucker.)

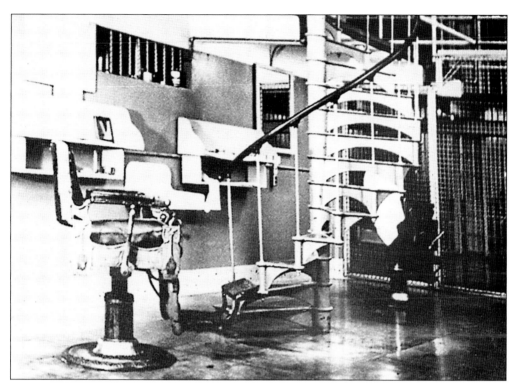

In this barber chair at Alcatraz, prisoners would give each other haircuts, which could be incredibly dangerous since prisoners had access to razors and scissors. One inmate murdered another by slitting his throat. Prisoner James Lucas once held a pair of barbershop scissors to Al Capone's throat, threatening him after he cut in line. Later, Lucas used another pair of scissors to stab Capone in the back, putting him in the hospital for a week. Below is the prison church. Religion was another privilege that prisoners were allotted. There was always a chaplain on duty for the prisoners and the guards. (Both, courtesy of Chuck Stucker.)

Above is the main communication booth of the prison. There were multiple listening devices, a duty station phone, a red emergency phone, and a speaker. The switchboard connected different lines throughout the island. There was also a boat frequency monitor, which was used to monitor boats coming to and passing by the island; a short-range radio; and a long-range radio. If any emergency occurred, this hub was key to receiving and directing orders in and out of the prison. The prison's shooting range is seen below. It was mandatory for all guards to be proficient with firearms. (Both, courtesy of Chuck Stucker.)

This was the main tower duty station on top of the prison roof. All of the prison's guard towers were equipped with armaments. This tower had a .30-caliber Winchester rifle with 50 rounds of ammunition and a Colt .45 semiautomatic pistol with three seven-round clips. This post became inactive in the later years of the prison. (Courtesy of Chuck Stucker.)

The second tower overlooked the dock. When the dock tower was first installed in 1933, it was connected to Building No. 64; this changed by 1941. From 1940 to 1941, the walkway was removed, and the entrance of the station was changed to a circular staircase. This station was armed with a .30-caliber Winchester rifle with 50 rounds of ammunition, a fully automatic Thompson gun (Tommy gun), a Colt .45 semiautomatic pistol with three seven-round clips, three gas grenades, and two gas masks. The dock tower overlooked everyone coming and going by ship. (Both, courtesy of Chuck Stucker.)

The powerhouse tower duty station was armed with a .30-caliber Winchester rifle with 50 rounds of ammunition, a Colt .45 semiautomatic pistol with three seven-round clips, three gas grenades, and a gas mask. (Courtesy of Chuck Stucker.)

The hill tower overlooked the area between the prison and the industry building and was armed with a .30-caliber Winchester rifle with 50 rounds of ammunition, a fully automatic Tommy gun, a Colt .45 semiautomatic pistol with three seven-round clips, three gas grenades, and a gas mask. This station connected to the walkway that led to the model tower at the far end of the island. (Courtesy of Chuck Stucker.)

The model tower was at the very end of the island. It was armed with a .30-caliber Winchester rifle with 50 rounds of ammunition, a Colt .45 semiautomatic pistol with three seven-round clips, one gas gun, six gas projectiles, and one gas mask. Once when three inmates attempted an escape, the guard in the model tower was forced to fire on the prisoners to stop them. (Courtesy of Chuck Stucker.)

The road tower was the most heavily armed station on the island and included a .30-caliber Winchester rifle with 50 rounds of ammunition, a fully automatic Tommy gun, a Colt .45 semiautomatic pistol with three seven-round clips, one gas gun with six rounds, six gas projectiles, and two gas masks. The road tower was connected to the prison recreation yard. Here, an officer walks between the two. The first person to attempt to escape from the island in 1936 was shot by the guard in the road tower. (Courtesy of the Golden Gate NRA Park Archives, Fred Cassidy Alcatraz Collection, GOGA 40024.038.)

Out with the old and in with the new. Many of the old Victorian military-era structures were torn down to make way for more modern buildings. Buildings Nos. 15 and 43, constructed during the 19th century, were demolished as part of the modernization of the island. (Courtesy of Chuck Stucker.)

The officers' quarters, originally built in 1881, had been adapted over the years but were obsolete by the 1940s and torn down. (Courtesy of Chuck Stucker.)

Above, giant letters on the roof identify Alcatraz to air traffic and indicate which direction is north. Such markings were common in the early days of aviation and helped pilots navigate. Pictured below is the inside of the island's power plant, built in 1912. The plant was essential to operations and provided all of the electricity on the island. (Both, courtesy of Chuck Stucker.)

The industry building is where most of the prisoners' production work was done, and the 1937–1938 warden's report shows the means of that production: "The model shop is a wood-working plant, very small, and employs but a few prisoners. It is doing good work in reconditioning furniture for government departments. A check of our daily labor reports shows that during the year 53.2 percent of the inmates were employed in the industries. We have no plan for money payment of prisoners. But, as an incentive to diligent labor those who are assigned to the industries are allowed from two to four days additional industrial credits per month in addition to the statutory good time deducted from their sentence." The laundry facilities seen below were also in the industry building. (Both, courtesy of Chuck Stucker.)

Alcatraz has no source of fresh water, and all water on the island is shipped in. There have been attempts to drill for fresh water, but with no success. The water tanks on the roof of the citadel, along with various in-ground water tanks, were used to store water during the military years. The new water tank that held the majority of the island's fresh water was built in 1940–1941 when the island was given a government grant for renovations. (Courtesy of Chuck Stucker.)

Above is the assistant warden/captain's duplex. Below are the family cottages. A 1937–1938 warden's report stated, "We have housing facilities for 51 families, with 28 rooms for single men and three additional quarters that we have been able to use in emergencies for single men. Two of these emergency quarters are located in the power plant and will not be available when we get under way with improvements contemplated in this building. All quarters have steam heat and all the family quarters are equipped with electric or gas ranges and refrigeration facilities. A number of the quarters for families are houses 50 years old, of poor construction, with plumbing and electric wiring not in accordance with present-day code standards. The remainder of the quarters are in good shape and are livable, although not all have modern plumbing and lighting." (Both, courtesy of Chuck Stucker.)

The image above shows the construction of buildings A, B, and C; below is a view of the final product. Known as the bachelors' quarters, they were built in 1940 in response to the need for more up-to-code officer housing. (This need was apparent in the 1937–1938 warden's report.) Occasionally, when family housing was in short supply, families would be housed in the bachelors' quarters. (Both, courtesy of Chuck Stucker.)

Work on the docks was daily and constant as laundry ships brought military uniforms to be cleaned by the prisoners. Most forts in the surrounding area had their laundry cleaned by the island facilities. Warden James Johnston describes the laundry operations along with the other services the island offered: "Under the guidance of the Federal Prison Industries, Incorporated, we operate a laundry, mat factory, clothing factory, model shop, and dry-cleaning plant. Our laundry and dry-cleaning plant service the US Transports, the Army posts in the San Francisco Bay area, and the Alcatraz penitentiary personnel. The mat factory receives most of its orders from the Navy Department. All of the mats produced are used on warships, principally those designated as the Pacific Fleet." There were shipments of diesel for the powerhouse to keep the electricity on the island going. The image below shows a laundry barge. (Both, courtesy of Chuck Stucker.)

At top is the *McDowell*, which was used in the 1930s and early 1940s as a transport to and from Alcatraz. An older ship, the *McDowell* was a 50-foot retired Army communication ship that sailed the English Channel during World War I. Gen. Irvin McDowell is pictured at right in 1866. He was commander of the Department of the Pacific in 1864. The *General Coxe*, seen above, named after Gen. Frank M. Coxe, was built in 1921 in West Virginia. The *Coxe* was one of the main transport ships to and from Alcatraz. (Above, both courtesy of Chuck Stucker. Right, office of the NPS Regional Historian. Courtesy of the Golden Gate NRA Park Archives, PAM Negative Collection, GOGA 35256.1483.)

Maj. Gen. I. McDowell
1866 — 1882

The *Warden Johnston*, namesake of James A. Johnston, was built from 1941 to 1944 by prisoners at McNeal Island under supervision of boat draftsmen Everet Soldin and Art "Woody" Woodruff. After its use on Alcatraz from 1945 to 1961, the Sea Scouts used the *Warden Johnston* for 35 years. It is currently privately owned and is considered a historic ship of San Francisco. (Courtesy of Chuck Stucker.)

The island is pictured here in the 1960s after the Federal Bureau of Prisons completed all its changes. It would remain this way until the 1970s. (Courtesy of Chuck Stucker.)

Three

LIFE AND TIMES OF THE NOTORIOUS

THE PRISONERS OF ALCATRAZ

The first federal prisoners on Alcatraz were 32 inmates left by the military for the Bureau of Prisons. The first large shipment of prisoners came by train cars aboard a barge transported to the island on August 22, 1934. This was followed by another barge of train cars, which brought the rest of the initial prisoners. For the next 29 years, Alcatraz would be home to some of America's most notorious criminals.

The prisoners who were sent to Alcatraz spent a majority of their time isolated. Each inmate had a single cell that was five feet by nine feet; prisoners did not share cells at Alcatraz. Prisoners were addressed by their last name only. Their day started at 7:00 a.m. and ended at 9:30 p.m. The day-to-day routine was precise and repetitive. Breakfast was served at 7:30 a.m., work began at 8:20 a.m., lunch break was at noon, and work resumed at 1:20 p.m. until 4:10 p.m. Dinner was at 4:40 p.m., and lights went out at 9:30 p.m. On Saturdays, Sundays, and holidays, inmates spent time in the recreation yard, where they were allowed to play baseball and other designated games. Twice a month, there would be a movie screening. Prisoners were allowed one visitor per month, and that person had to be approved by the warden. All of these amenities were privileges that could be revoked. The only rights a prisoner had were food, water, shelter, and medical care.

This isolation resulted in many escape attempts—a total of 36 over a 29-year period. None of the attempts were considered successful, although five prisoners have never been found and are listed as missing and presumed drowned. Out of 34 men who attempted to escape (two tried twice), two were found drowned and six were shot and killed. The others were all recaptured shortly after their escape and returned to the prison.

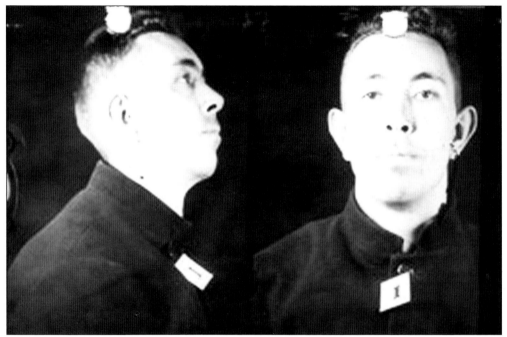

From an alphabetical listing, Frank Bolt became the first prisoner on Alcatraz. Numbered 001, he was one of the 32 prisoners left by the military for the Department of Justice. Bolt was in prison for committing sodomy. He was sentenced to the maximum of five years, with parole scheduled for September 25, 1934, only three months and six days after being transferred. (Courtesy of Chuck Stucker.)

Here is a photograph of the first trainload of federal prisoners sent to Alcatraz. This was technically the third influx of prisoners to the island. The first were the military prisoners, followed by a small number of prisoners used as a practice run to prepare the guards for the large shipments of prisoners. There would be one more shipment to complete the initial prison population. (Courtesy of Chuck Stucker.)

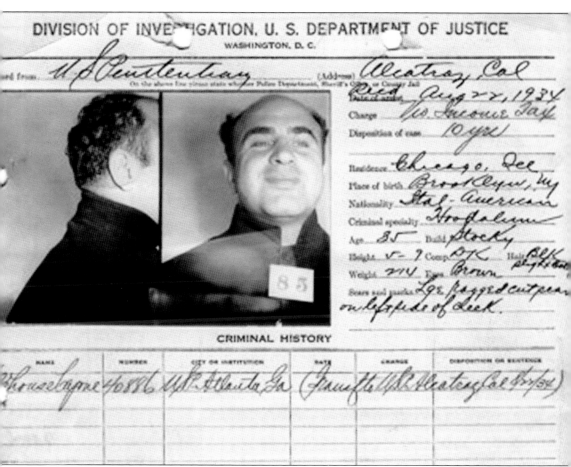

Alphonse Gabriel Capone, inmate No. 085, was known to most as Al "Scarface" Capone. He was one of the most infamous prisoners who ever stepped foot on Alcatraz. Transferred to the island in the first trainload of prisoners in 1934, he came from the federal penitentiary in Atlanta, Georgia. Capone was serving 11 years for tax evasion. Prior to his imprisonment, he was one of America's most infamous organized crime kingpins. Starting his criminal career in New York and later moving to Chicago, Capone made an empire out of bootlegging, casinos, speakeasies, and countless other criminal activities. He orchestrated one of the most famous gangland murders of the 1920s, the St. Valentine's Day Massacre. While at Alcatraz, Capone became known by some as a rat, resulting in attempts on his life. The most brutal attempt was by fellow inmate James Lucas, who stabbed Capone in the back. Capone's stay on Alcatraz lasted until January 6, 1939. (Courtesy of Chuck Stucker.)

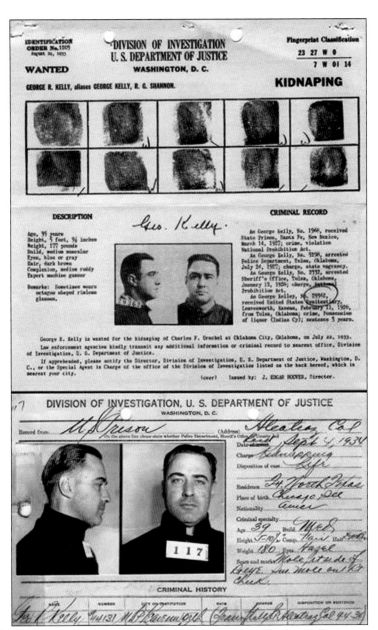

"Machine Gun" Kelly, inmate No. 117, whose actual name was George Kelly Barnes, was another of Alcatraz's most famous prisoners. His criminal life began soon after he was separated from his first wife, Geneva Ramsey. He worked for a time as a cab driver but found steady work as a bootlegger. Kelly gained his true prominence as a criminal after meeting his second wife, Kathryn Thorne. His rise to "public enemy number one" was partially due to Kathryn's boasting about him in different crime circles. His demise came from kidnapping Charles Urschel, a wealthy businessman, in July 1933. After receiving the ransom for Urschel and spending a short time on the lam, Kelly was captured. Convicted of kidnapping, he was sentenced to life. He was transferred to Alcatraz in 1934 after telling reporters he would break out of Leavenworth, Kansas. During his stay at Alcatraz, he was well behaved, and in 1951, he was transferred from Alcatraz back to Leavenworth, where he died of a heart attack. (Courtesy of Chuck Stucker.)

DIVISION OF INVESTIGATION, U. S. DEPARTMENT OF JUSTICE
WASHINGTON, D. C.

rd from: _M S Prison_ (Address _Alcatraz Cal_

On the above line please state whether Police Department, Sheriff's Office, or County Jail

Date of arrest: _Rec'd Sept 4, 1934_

Charge: _Robbery & Assault_

Disposition of case: _30 years_

Residence: _San Francisco Cal_

Place of birth: _same_

Nationality: _Amer_

Criminal specialty: _____

Age: _32_ Build: _Small_

Height: _5-5_ Comp: _Han_ Hair: _Bw_

Weight: _165_ Eyes: _Bw_

Scars and marks: _Lg cut scar on upper lip. Lap cut scar on left cheek_

CRIMINAL HISTORY

NAME	NUMBER	CITY OR INSTITUTION	DATE	CHARGE	DISPOSITION OR SENTENCE
Charles Berta	_39571_	_U.S.P. Leavenworth Kans_		_(Transf to U.S.P. Alcatraz Cal 9-4-34)_	

(Please furnish all additional criminal history and police record on separate sheet)

Charles "Charlie" Berta, also known as "Harry Stone," was inmate No. 132. Alcatraz guard Ed Stucker said Berta was the "toughest man he had ever met." Berta was first arrested in 1920 for stealing a car when he was 18. Later, he was arrested for robbing a bank in Canada and served eight years in a Canadian prison. He was arrested again in the United States for robbing a mail car and assaulting the messenger, for which he was sentenced to 25 years. While serving his 25-year sentence at the federal penitentiary in Leavenworth, he attempted an escape. For his part in the escape attempt, five years were added to his sentence, for a total of 30 years. He was transferred to Alcatraz, where he spent some of those years before being paroled in 1949. (Courtesy of Chuck Stucker.)

DIVISION OF INVESTIGATION, U. S. DEPARTMENT OF JUSTICE
WASHINGTON, D. C.

Institution...... **UNITED STATES PENITENTIARY** .... Located at...... **ALCATRAZ, CALIFORNIA**

Received...	**AUGUST 6, 1936**
From	**USP. LEAVENWORTH, KANSAS**
Crime	**CONSP. TO KIDNAP & TRANSPO**
Sentence:	**LIFE** yrs. mos.
Date of sentence....	**JULY 27, 1936**
Sentence begins......	**July 27, 1936**
Sentence expires......	**LIFE**
Good time sentence expires......	**LIFE**
Date of birth.**9/10/09** Occupation	**Bakers**
Birthplace.**Canada** Nationality	**Canadi**
Age.....**29** Comp.	**Fair**
Height...**70 inches** Eyes	**Blue**
Weight....**137 lbs.** Hair	**Light Brow**
Build....**Slim**	

Scars and marks...**"V" shaped scar index finger left hand; Operation scars right & left side ab** ears; operation scars on all fingers of each hand.

CRIMINAL HISTORY

Alvin Francis Karpowicz (or Karpis), also known as "Creepy," was inmate No. 325. Creepy Karpis started his life of crime at the age of 10. A leader of the Baker-Karpis gang, his reputation grew in the criminal world. His downfall came with his conviction for kidnapping millionaire William Hamm Jr. of Hamm's Brewing Company. He served almost 26 years on Alcatraz, from late 1936 to 1962, after which he was sent to McNeil Island Federal Penitentiary in Washington State, where he came to know Charles Manson prior to Manson's 1960s murder conspiracy with the Manson family. After being paroled in 1969, Karpis was deported to Canada. He later published his memoirs. (Courtesy of Chuck Stucker.)

Robert Franklin Stroud, inmate No. 594, was known as "the Birdman." Stroud was one of the most, if not the most, famous inmate to ever serve time on Alcatraz. Unlike Burt Lancaster's portrayal in the film *Birdman of Alcatraz*, Stroud was a murderer who many considered a psychopath and never had any birds on Alcatraz. His first sentence was for manslaughter after shooting a bartender to death. He spent the first part of his life in prison at McNeil Island Federal Penitentiary in Washington State, later being transferred to Leavenworth because of his aggressive behavior toward inmates and prison staff. While at Leavenworth, he brutally stabbed a guard to death and was convicted of murder and sentenced to be hanged. His mother was able to plead his case to Pres. Woodrow Wilson, who reduced his sentence to life without parole. Warden T.W. Morgan put Stroud in permanent solitary confinement because of his violent tendencies. He was transferred to Alcatraz in 1942, where he spent 17 years—6 in isolation and 11 in the infirmary. During his life in prison, Stroud wrote two books concerning canary diseases. He died in a prisoner medical facility in Springfield, Missouri, in 1963. (Courtesy of Chuck Stucker.)

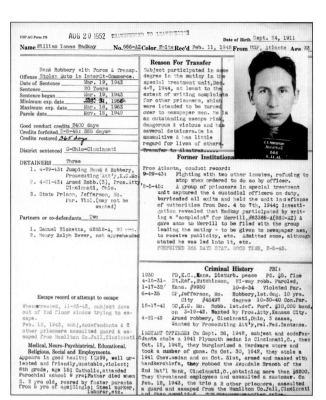

William "Willie" Isaac Radkay, inmate No. 666, was one of Kansas City's most notorious armed robbers and later, a favorite at Alcatraz reunions. Transferred from the federal penitentiary in Atlanta, he spent time on Alcatraz from 1945 to 1952 with some of the most infamous inmates. After being released from Alcatraz, Radkay reformed and wrote an autobiography, *The Devil Incarnate: From Altar Boy to Alcatraz*. (Courtesy of Chuck Stucker.)

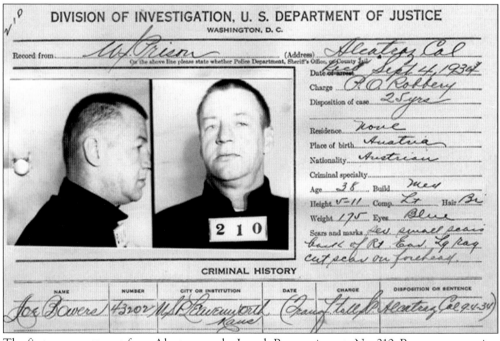

The first escape attempt from Alcatraz was by Joseph Bowers, inmate No. 210. Bowers was serving a 25-year sentence for robbery. In April 1936, he attempted to climb the fence at the edge of the island. Refusing to stop after being ordered, he was shot and fell to his death. (Courtesy of Chuck Stucker.)

DIVISION OF INVESTIGATION, U. S. DEPARTMENT OF JUSTICE
WASHINGTON, D. C.

Institution... *U.S Penitentiary* ... Located at... *Alcatraz Jsl Calif*

Received... OCT 26 1935 ... *Rawfr*

From... *U.S.P. Leavenworth Kans*

Crime... *conspto to transport kidnapfper*

Sentence: *Life* yrs. ... mos. ... days

Date of sentence... *5-17-35*

Sentence begins... *5-17-35*

Sentence expires... *Life*

Good time sentence expires... *Life*

Date of birth *6-4-99* Occupation... *Painter*

Birthplace... *Mo* Nationality *Amer*

Age... *36* Comp... *Ruddy*

Height... *5-5* Eyes... *Brown*

Weight... *150* Hair... *Dk Bn*

Build... *Sm Med*

Scars and marks... *1½" scar, 2" long under left ear* ... *1½" scar, under left ear*

CRIMINAL HISTORY

NAME	NUMBER	CITY OR INSTITUTION	DATE	CHARGE	DISPOSITION ON SENTENCE
Arth R Barker	*46978*	*USP Leav, Kans*	*5-15-35*	*Consp to Kidnap*	*Life*

Arthur Barker, also known as "Doc" Barker, inmate No. 268, was sentenced to Alcatraz for the kidnapping of Edward G. Bremer. He attempted to escape in January 1939 with four accomplices—William Martin, Rufus McCain, Dale Stamphill, and Henry Young. They were caught at the island's shoreline where Barker and Stamphill were shot for refusing to surrender. Barker later died from his wounds. The rest were returned to their cells. (Courtesy of Chuck Stucker.)

John K. Giles, inmate No. 250, was transferred to Alcatraz in 1935. For 10 years, Giles worked in the Army laundry, taking small pieces of uniforms to create one for himself. On Tuesday, July 31, 1945, Giles boarded the transport *Coxe* in his uniform, hoping to head for San Francisco; however, he ended up on Angel Island where he was captured and returned to Alcatraz. Here, he poses in his uniform after capture. (Courtesy of Chuck Stucker.)

ALCATRAZ ISLAND OFFICERS

"RIOT OF 1946"

Warden J. A. Johnston   **Associate Warden E. J. Miller**

B.A. Burch   J.U. Burdett   C.G. Fish   I. B. Faulk   E. Lageson

J.H. Simpson   E.F. Stucker   C. W. Sundstrom   H.W. Weinhold

The "Battle for Alcatraz" or "Alcatraz Blastout" was the bloodiest escape attempt that Alcatraz ever saw. On May 2–4, 1946, six prisoners attempted to take control of the island. Clarence Carnes, Bernard Coy, Joe Cretzer, Marvin Hubbard, Sam Shockley, and Miran Thompson overpowered guards and gained control of the cell house. Two officers, William Miller and Harold Stites, were killed, and 18 others were injured. The US Marines were called in, and Alcatraz was retaken. When the smoke cleared, Coy, Cretzer, and Hubbard were found dead. Carnes, Shockley, and Thompson were tried for the murders of the two guards. Shockley and Thompson were executed. Carnes was sentenced to another life sentence because he was only 19. Above are some of the officers at the time. Below are, from left to right, Coy, Hubbard, and Cretzer. (Both, courtesy of Chuck Stucker.)

The most elaborate escape attempt from Alcatraz was committed on June 11, 1962, by Frank Lee Morris and his accomplices, brothers John and Clarence Anglin and fellow inmate Allen Clayton West. Their plan took almost seven months. Over that period, they excavated openings to the ventilation ducts in their cells. On June 11, they made their escape. (West was left behind because he could not get the grill covering his ventilation duct off.) They eluded detection from the night count by using dummy heads they made from a variety of items collected from the prison, which they covered in hair from the barbershop. Morris and the Anglin brothers were never found and are listed as missing and presumed drowned. Pictured are Morris and the Anglin brothers. (Courtesy of Chuck Stucker.)

When prisoners were not attempting to escape, they were either in their cells, at work, or in the recreation yard, although they were only allowed in the yard twice a week—on Saturday and Sunday. Above is one of the most famous photographs of prisoners in the yard, from 1950. Most are unidentified, but there are a few infamous men playing dominos—John R. McDowell, the man with the visor in back; Willie Radkay, facing the camera at left; and Machine Gun Kelly, sitting next to him. Baseball was another favorite pastime of the inmates. Below, prisoners are playing a game in the 1940s. (Both, courtesy of Chuck Stucker.)

PENCIL DRAWING
of
AL CAPONE
85 ALCATRAZ
ISLAND

DREW BY AN
CONVICT of ALCATRAZ
ISLAND

Art by prison inmates was a common thing. An Alcatraz inmate created the drawing of Al Capone seen above. The drawing at right was in response to a letter sent out by Lieutenant Culver regarding the cat nuisance on the island. The letter was to "remind owners that all cats must remain inside their own residences or teach them how to swim, as all cats running loose will be gotten rid of in some manner, shape or form." This did not pertain to the prisoners, but they must have found out about it, and Izzy, whose last name is unknown, decided to draw a sketch of the whole mater. This was sometime between 1933 and 1936 while the Bay Bridge was still under construction. (Both, courtesy of Chuck Stucker.)

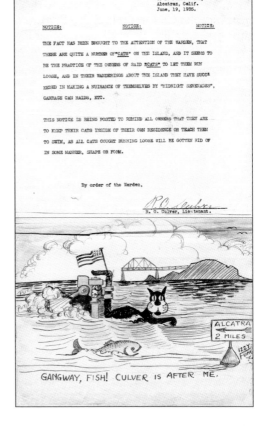

James Pivaroff, inmate No. 276, was also known as "Dip" because he would pickpocket items from guests if given the opportunity. Transferred from McNeil Island Federal Penitentiary in Washington State, Pivaroff was doing time for postal robbery and assault. Before his transfer, Frank Loveland, the supervisor of classification, wrote, "Transferred to Alcatraz was recommended with the notation that it is felt that he is a vicious type, deliberate and cool." Here, he is playing guitar for another inmate. Like many things, music was a privilege given at various times. Eventually, the prisoners would get a music hour every evening. (Courtesy of Chuck Stucker.)

The Rock Islanders was a group of prisoners who played music as a privilege. The band had rotating musicians, depending on who was currently paroled. Al Capone played banjo for the band for some years. They would play Sunday concerts and special events on the island. At right is the cover of a program that included the lineup for the Sunday concert on April 28, 1935. At that time, Capone was in the band. The photograph above shows the Rock Islanders in rehearsal. The band was a staple on the island until the prison closed. (Both, courtesy of Chuck Stucker.)

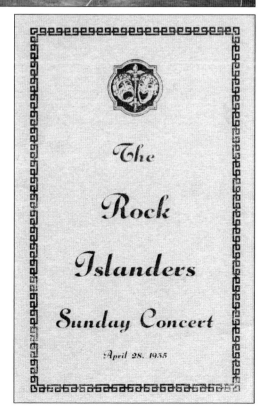

The

Rock

Islanders

Sunday Concert

April 28, 1935

Smoking was another privilege that inmates enjoyed. These pouches were used by inmates and held Bull Durham tobacco. No outside tobacco products were allowed for use by the inmates, only what was distributed by the prison officials. If prisoners were caught with commercial tobacco, they would be punished. (Courtesy of Chuck Stucker.)

Good work and behavior are what gave these prisoners their privileges. This photograph shows prisoners at work in the bakery, with a guard standing close by. Most of the guards and prisoners went about their daily routines together without problems, and in some cases, they would even pose for pictures. (Courtesy of Chuck Stucker.)

The prisoners also made cargo nets as part of their production work. The nets were used for loading cargo on and off the ships that came to the island. (Courtesy of Chuck Stucker.)

Here are prisoners unloading food. Today, this is the exit of the prison block bookstore. (Courtesy of Chuck Stucker.)

In 1963, the prison was finally shut down for good. The Federal Bureau of Prisons cited costly operations and dilapidation as the excuses for shutting down Alcatraz. The inmates were transported to other prisons around the country. In the end, the island had 1,546 prisoners over 29 years. These were the last of the prisoners leaving the island. On his way out, prisoner Frank Weatherman caught the ear of reporters saying, "Alcatraz was no good for nobody." (Courtesy of Chuck Stucker.)

Over its 29-year existence, there were 1,576 prisoner numbers issued, but only 1,546 prisoners. The extra 30 numbers came from prisoners who served two sentences on Alcatraz, meaning they committed another federal crime after completing their first sentence. Theodore James Audett, also known as "Blackie," had three different numbers assigned to him. (Courtesy of Chuck Stucker.)

Four

WATCHING OVER THE ISLAND—WARDENS, GUARDS, AND PERSONNEL

1934–1963

The first warden of Alcatraz was James A. Johnston. He handpicked his associate warden, Cecil Shuttleworth, and the guards. These men were the first federal officers to serve on the island. There were also men who served as unarmed clerks, performing different duties around the island. The guards and their families lived on the island for the duration of their duty.

Over the years, the guards were paid different amounts. According to historian Michael Esslinger, "In 1934 the average annual salary of a correctional officer at Alcatraz was $3,162 and, by the time the prison closed . . . nearly $5,000 a year." There was a six-percent deduction for retirement and income taxes each year. Salaries were based on a 40-hour workweek made up of five eight-hour shifts. Guards were given a 10-percent increase for shifts worked between 6:00 p.m. and 6:00 a.m. Holiday pay was double the normal rate, and officers were offered meals at 25¢.

Officers were charged rent to live on the island. The cost for an officer living in the bachelors' quarters was $10 a month, including personal laundry service. Guards with families would live in the larger family quarters, where officers were charged $20 to $43 a month plus another dollar for laundry service. No pets or "intoxicating beverages" were allowed on the island.

The guards' lives were not just filled with duty. A lot of their time on the island was spent with their families and other guards. The camaraderie among the guards and their families shows a different perspective of life on Alcatraz.

James A. Johnston was the first warden of Alcatraz. He was selected by the attorney general, Homer S. Cummings. Johnston had a long track record when it came to prison management in California. He first served a short stint as warden at Folsom Prison from 1912 to 1913. He moved on to become the warden of San Quentin until 1925. During these years, he gained the nickname "Golden Rule Warden" and received much praise for removing prisoners' striped uniforms and using their labor for public works projects. After a short break from the prison system to venture into the private sector, Johnston was called back to duty. From his previous achievements, the Department of Justice considered Johnston to be a scientific penologist and best suited to run the new maximum-security prison on Alcatraz. He remained there until his retirement in 1946. (Courtesy of the Golden Gate NRA Park Archives, Interpretation Negative Collection, GOGA 2316.)

This photograph, taken in 1934, shows a portion of the initial guard staff on the island. The names of the officers are written on the photograph, but are difficult to read. The man seated at center in the suit and light-colored hat is Warden Johnston. To his right is associate warden Cecil Shuttleworth. (Courtesy of Chuck Stucker.)

Isaac "Ike" Faulk, born January 15, 1899, was another of the first guards on Alcatraz, beginning work on the island on June 19, 1934, when he was 35. He and his wife, Esther, and their three children lived on the island until 1953, when he retired. (Courtesy of Chuck Stucker.)

Edward J. Miller was another of the initial correctional officers, arriving June 23, 1934. His career on Alcatraz lasted until 1947. He climbed the ranks to become associate warden of Alcatraz by the time he left. He lived on the island with his wife, Rose. (Courtesy of Chuck Stucker.)

Starting in 1934, Walter Dorington worked as an officer on the island. This picture from the late 1930s shows Dorington at his desk. The wall behind him separates him from the armory. One day, while at work, a misfire sent a bullet directly toward this wall, striking it right where Dorington's head was. The shot resulted in a large bulge in the wall, but Dorington was uninjured. A little shaken, he stood up from his desk, grabbed his lunch, and simply walked home, returning to work the next day. Sadly, Dorington passed away on the island in 1947 from natural causes. (Courtesy of Chuck Stucker.)

All of the inmates' mail was censored for content. Robert Russell Baker worked as the mail censor for Alcatraz; he came to the island when he was 27 years old in 1937. He remained for 23 years, until 1957, when he retired at the age of 50. Here, he is at work in 1949. Below is a letter from Alcatraz going to Modesto, California. The stamp on the left side was to authenticate the origin of letter and let the recipient know where it was coming from. (Both, courtesy of Chuck Stucker.)

Nova Stucker is seen here after a good day of fishing on Alcatraz. Nova first came to the island with his wife, Edna, in 1934 to help with the initial influx of prisoners. He remained about a year, until 1935, when he left to pursue further career advancement at Leavenworth in Kansas. Nova returned to Alcatraz in 1949 as captain, remaining until 1952, when he left as associate warden and went to McNeil Island in Washington State. (Courtesy of Chuck Stucker.)

Seen here are Edward Stucker (left) and Emil Rychner. Rychner, the senior officer, worked on the island from 1935 until 1961, when he retired. Stucker worked from 1939 until 1953, when he also retired. His years were mostly consecutive except for when he took a short break from Alcatraz to serve in World War II. He was the brother of Nova Stucker and was involved in the 1946 "Battle for Alcatraz." (Courtesy of Chuck Stucker.)

Marshall Rose worked as an officer on Alcatraz for 16 years. He lived on the island with his wife, Vi, from 1936 until 1952, when he retired. Rose is seen here in the first version of the prison guards' uniform. The formal black uniform, removed from service in the late 1930s due to their almost ostentatious appearance, was replaced by an all-gray uniform with a red tie. The new uniforms resulted in the prisoners giving the guards the nickname "red ties." (Courtesy of Chuck Stucker.)

After 24 years of service as a guard, Clifford Fish retired from Alcatraz one year before its closure in 1962. In 1999 video footage, Fish claimed that he was one of the only known guards to get into a hand-to-hand fight with "the Birdman," Robert Shroud. He said, "We took him down to get a shower . . . I had turned to look at something and Mike [fellow officer] was not paying much attention . . . we did not expect much trouble . . . and he [Stroud] took the lid of the toilet and hit Mike over the head with it, knocked him out . . . he swung at me and I ducked him . . . we went at it hammer and claw and I finally got the hammer lock on him . . . Mike got up . . . we said, 'you son of a bitch you're going to get your bath now . . . cold water, no warm bath.' " (Courtesy of Chuck Stucker.)

Alcatraz had a number of pastors. One was Byron Elias Eshelman (right), who held the post from 1946 to 1949. He was married to Anne Eshelman. The chaplain on Alcatraz was on the Classification Committee with the warden and chief medical officer. The committee analyzed each prisoner's progress over a certain period and decided what steps were needed to help rehabilitate them. Above is a prisoner art exhibit at Union Square. On the left is the director of exhibits, Frans Bergmann, with another chaplain, Wayne Lindsay Hunter, who served from 1936 to 1939. (Both, courtesy of Chuck Stucker.)

Louis Nelson was a guard on Alcatraz from 1941 to 1944. He then joined the Navy in World War II. After witnessing the 1946 "Battle for Alcatraz," he returned to the island from 1946 to 1948. In a later interview he said, "I was not going back in prison work. I was sick of prisons, as most people were. Then they had the riot on Alcatraz and I just decided that since they were having trouble there, and needed help, I'd better go back and help, even though I had another job lined up." Nelson, better known as "Red" Nelson, went on to be warden at San Quentin. (Courtesy of Chuck Stucker.)

Warden Edwin B. Swope replaced Warden Johnston after his retirement. Swope had a long history in the warden's chair. He had served four other prisons in New Mexico, Washington, Indiana, and Colorado. Swope could be hard on the prisoners, demanding obedience for his rules; however, the returns for obedience were increased privileges. Along with extended visitations and more recreation time, Swope gave prisoners a variety of incentives for good behavior. He increased inmate movie times from once a month to twice a month and allowed the occasional Western or military flick. The guards were another story, as many of his new rules met resistance from them. (Courtesy of the Golden Gate NRA Park Archives, Weed/McPherson Family Alcatraz Photograph Collection, GOGA 35178.)

George DeVincenzi is one of the voices on the modern cellblock tour of Alcatraz. He was hired as a guard in 1951 and worked on the island for six years. He was ordered to the hospital wing, where at times he played chess with Robert Stroud. He said, "I could only play a game of chess with Stroud if the West Gun Gallery Officer was a friend of mine . . . the officer peered through the window . . . to ensure I was ok." The officer had to be DeVincenzi's friend because recreational interaction with the inmates was strictly prohibited. In this photograph are, from left to right, DeVincenzi, unidentified, Emil Rychner, and George Gregory. (Courtesy of the Golden Gate NRA Park Archives, Carl Sundstrom Alcatraz Photo Collection, GOGA 3264.)

Paul Madigan became warden in 1955, replacing Edwin B. Swope. Unlike his predecessors, Madigan came up through the ranks of Alcatraz itself, first as a lieutenant, then captain, then associate warden, and finally reaching the pinnacle of warden. Madigan had been through it all, which created a new kind of leadership. He became known as the diplomatic warden who could meet the needs of the prisoners as well as his staff. His guard staff, however, did call him "Promising Paul" because he made promises he never kept. He attended Mass with the prisoners and was a devout Catholic. In 1961, he was transferred as warden to McNeil Island in Washington. He is pictured here with his wife in the warden's house around 1956. (Courtesy of Chuck Stucker.)

Associate Warden Olin Guy Blackwell, "Blackie" to most, became warden upon the departure of Paul Madigan. It was 1961; Blackwell would only have a two-year run as warden. Left with a dilapidated prison and low funds to run it, Blackwell was facing an uphill battle, which would soon be lost as Alcatraz was shut down in 1963. This is not to say that Blackwell did not serve well. He was considered by the staff to be "warm." Blackwell lightened the rules for the prisoners, allowing more radio programs and more literature that once had been banned. Blackwell's reputation was tarnished when Clarence and John Anglin, Frank Morris, and Allen West executed the most elaborate escape the island had ever seen. (Courtesy of the Golden Gate NRA Park Archives, Maurice Ordway Papers, GOGA 35335.13.)

Aside from the prisoners and guards, Alcatraz had a number of clerks who worked on the island doing the day-to-day paperwork and other jobs. The clerks commuted by boat every day. Pictured here are some of the clerks around 1940 (from left to right): Bones, Baldwin, Keefe, Berg, Gaynor, Kaeppel, Washington, and Sundstrom. (Courtesy of Chuck Stucker.)

Training was something all officers had to do; defending themselves against some of the toughest criminals in America was no easy job. Here are some officers after a workout. From left to right are unidentified, Jack Daly, Ed Stucker, Emil Rychner, and Phillip Bergen. (Courtesy of Chuck Stucker.)

There were other kinds of officers on Alcatraz during World War II—military ones. As some guards left to serve their country in the war, the war came to Alcatraz. Above, the military loads an antiaircraft gun on the roof of the prison. On the right is Marshall Rose, impersonating Napoleon, as the military personnel hoist up the cannon. The men who served on Alcatraz defending San Francisco from bombing are seen below. Once again, Alcatraz was a fortress, even if it was only for a short time. (Above, courtesy of Chuck Stucker; below, courtesy Golden Gate NRA Park Archives, Interpretation Negative Collection, GOGA 2316.)

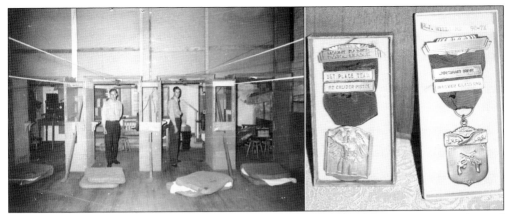

Keeping up with target practice was required of the officers. The shooting range was located above the old sally port. At left, the guys are squeezing off some rounds. Accuracy was key, and the officers would receive medals based on competitions with other prison guards in off-island competitions. At right are two medals won by R.J. Willard. (Courtesy of Chuck Stucker.)

Alcatraz was not business all the time; there was also time for recreational activity. Guards would spend much of their time outside of work with other guards, participating in all kinds of activities and sports. These officers were members of a choir and are seen here at practice. From left to right are Louis Nelson, ? Scanland, Marvin Orr, and ? Hurley. (Courtesy of Chuck Stucker.)

The guards would mingle both on the island and off. Here, some officers participate as part of a bowling team. From left to right are Don Martin, Emil Rychner, George Black, Bob Stoute, and Bret Bode. (Courtesy of Chuck Stucker.)

The guards also liked to play golf. Here are a couple of officers out on the links. From left to right are Burns, Herbert, Jim Comerford, and Emil Rychner. (Courtesy of Chuck Stucker.)

All the officers, clerks, and their families gathered at the officers' lounge for the retirement of Warden James Johnston. Such gatherings were not uncommon. (Courtesy of Chuck Stucker.)

These officers had a great day fishing as they brought home a large take of bass in 1956. (Courtesy of Chuck Stucker.)

There were always special guests coming to the island. Near the end of World War II, some of the Bataan Death March survivors came to the island. They had survived one of the most brutal war crimes committed in the Pacific, and now they were home touring Alcatraz. Pictured are, from left to right, Sgt. John O. Morning, associate warden Edward Miller, and Corp. John W. Knight. The writing on the top of the photograph reads, "James A. Johnston Warden US Penitentiary-Alcatraz March 24th 1945 Engraved for Serg. John O Morning and Cpl. John A. Knight." (Courtesy of Chuck Stucker.)

Associate warden Edward Miller was introduced to some of the best early-20th-century baseball pitchers. From left to right are Herb Pennock, Miller, and Harry Warren "Rip" Collins. Pennock played for the Philadelphia Athletics, Boston Red Sox, and the New York Yankees. He won at least one World Series championship with each team—three with the Yankees. Rip Collins was a star pitcher for the Yankees, Red Sox, and Detroit Tigers. (Courtesy of Chuck Stucker.)

Associate warden Edward Miller was not the only person who got to meet star athletes. Here, basketball stars William Fenton "Bill" Russell and K.C. Jones visit Alcatraz. From left to right are Russell, George DeVincenzi, Jones, Emil Rychner, and Fr. Richard Joseph Scanell. At the time, Russell and Jones were playing for the University of San Francisco, leading the Dons to 60 consecutive victories and two NCAA championships. In 1956, Russell went on to win a gold medal in basketball at the Melbourne Olympic games. Later that year, he was drafted by the Boston Celtics, becoming one of the greatest centers of all time, winning 11 NBA championships, becoming a five-time MVP, and making 12 all-star appearances. K.C. Jones also attended the 1956 Melbourne Olympics, winning a gold medal with Russell. He also played for Boston, winning eight championships. (Courtesy of Chuck Stucker.)

Five

WIVES, SONS, AND DAUGHTERS OF ALCATRAZ

110 YEARS OF FAMILY LIFE

Many of the personnel who worked on Alcatraz from its days as a fortress until it closed in 1963 had families who lived on the island with them. The lives of these wives, sons, and daughters are many times overshadowed by popular history of the fortress guns, prison cells, prisoners, and escapes, though it was the lives of these families on the island that brought it from a gloomy, cold, concrete prison island in the bay to a place full of life and vibrancy.

The families living on Alcatraz created a neighborhood just like any other in America, perhaps even more unified. When reflecting on life on Alcatraz, Chuck Stucker said, "It was probably similar to a military base, there were some rules to be followed and some places you just could not go." Aside from the rules, the children all went to school together, played together on and off the island, and in some cases, married each other later in life. The wives organized events on the island. There was a wives' club, and many of the families spent holidays together. Some of the wives worked as the Sunday school teachers. Even though they came from different backgrounds, living on Alcatraz gave them commonality.

The lighthouse keepers, the doctor, and the wardens all had families on the island as well, only they lived near the prison above the parade ground. These families, like everyone else, mingled with the guards' families and were part of the Alcatraz community. The only distinction was that the kids who lived on the parade ground were known as "the topside kids" because they lived above the other children.

Throughout the different stages of Alcatraz, there has almost always been family life. Children might not have always been living on the island, but for decades, photographs of wives have appeared. Here, wives of military officers are pictured in the 19th-century garden next to the citadel. (Courtesy of Chuck Stucker.)

This photograph from 1882 shows the lighthouse keeper and his wife. (Courtesy of the Golden Gate NRA Park Archives, PAM Negative Collection, GOGA 35256.0537.)

Bessie Crabbe and George G. Gatley are pictured sometime before they were married. Gatley was a second lieutenant of Battery D, Fifth Artillery, West Point class of 1890. He met Crabbe while stationed at the Presidio. Her father was a longtime officer of Alcatraz. Here, the bride and groom pose outside Alcatraz's fortress walls. From left to right are two unidentified; the Alcatraz commander; Lt. Col. Francis Guenther; three unidentified; Capt. George Crabbe; Bessie Crabbe; and 2nd Lt. George Gatley. (Courtesy of Faeylyn Wylder-Lackey.)

Here is a view of military officers and their wives in 1902. In the background, the *General McPherson* can be seen. (Courtesy of the Golden Gate NRA Park Archives, Office of Resource Management Alcatraz Collection, GOGA 18346.230.)

By the 1920s, family life on Alcatraz was changing, and more children were appearing. Here, a military inmate known only as Mason holds Kenneth Mickelwaite. Baseball was always a favorite of inmates during the federal penitentiary years and continued to be popular during the early 1920s as well. The "A" on Mason's hat most likely stood for Alcatraz. (Courtesy Fred Cassidy Collection and the Golden Gate NRA Park Archives, Kenneth Mickelwaite Alcatraz Collection, GOGA 32473.01.)

Three generations of women on Alcatraz pose next to a cannon in the late 1920s. In the center is Edith Lynch with her aunt and friend. (Courtesy of Chuck Stucker.)

"The Big House"
UNIQUE AND PRACTICAL

Above is Building No. 64 after the transition to federal penitentiary. Many of the families on Alcatraz lived here and called it the "Big House." There were also other places on the island where families could live. At right is a photograph of Esther Faulk (second row, far right), wife of guard Isaac Faulk. The Faulk family lived in the large Victorian house directly behind them. Esther wrote poetry about the island in the 1930s (see page 114). (Both, courtesy of Chuck Stucker.)

The Faulks were one of the first families on the island. Ed Faulk would later recollect, "It was the best time of my life . . . You ask any of the kids my age, and they will say there was no place they would rather be brought up than there." Here is Isaac Faulk with his children (from left to right) Herb, Ed, and Ruth during Easter 1938. (Courtesy of Chuck Stucker.)

From left to right are some of the guards' wives around 1935, Margaret Dorington, Ed Faulk, Esther Faulk, Mrs. Burch, Mrs. Stewart, Mrs. Perendel, Mrs. Candestry, Mrs. Bragg, and Mrs. Roman. (Courtesy of Chuck Stucker.)

Ida May Johnston, wife of Warden Johnston, is seen here posing with a fishing pole and some bass that officers had caught. Ida and James had been married for 29 years by the time Alcatraz opened. (Courtesy of Chuck Stucker.)

Fishing on the island was a great hobby for the kids as well as the officers. Chuck Stucker used to fish off the island every day after school. His father gave him prisoners' tobacco pouches to hold bait and make weights. Chuck, seen here with his uncle Nova holding a line of capzone in the late 1940s, said that these were his "favorite fish to catch off the island." (Courtesy of Chuck Stucker.)

Aside from fishing, roller-skating was another popular activity for the kids. One child recollected in the Alcatraz alumni newsletter, "The kids used to roller skate all the way from the lighthouse, down the hill and around the curves in the road. Sparks shot out as skates whizzed along the cement." (Courtesy of Chuck Stucker.)

Roller skates were great fun until bikes were permitted on the island in the late 1940s. Here, Sandy Nelson (second from right) poses with three friends who lived on the island. (Courtesy of Chuck Stucker.)

The kids also had their own Alcatraz playgrounds. Pictured here is the old playground that was removed around 1940. On the front seesaw are, from left to right, Charlie Ping, Joan Mickelson, Ralph Preshaw (lying down), Marylyn Preshaw (in back), ? Preshaw, Freddie Baker, and unidentified. Identified on the back seesaw are Dorothy Dorington and Lucille Kline. (Courtesy of Chuck Stucker.)

The playground with the seesaws was only known to a handful of the kids on the island, as it was replaced around 1940 with a new playground. Children would also come to know this sandbox and swing set as a playground around 1950. (Courtesy of Chuck Stucker.)

Here are the men and women who taught Sunday school to the children around 1938. From left to right are Mary Ping, Julia Boyd, Tracy Heath, Chaplain Hunter, Mrs. Hunter, Ruth Chandler, Bea Rychner, and Marion Simpson. (Courtesy of Chuck Stucker.)

There were children of all ages on the island. The kindergartners pictured here are, from left to right, C. Neally, Harry Snyder, Jerry McDiene, Arthur Star, P. Gaynor, C. Albrecht, Phyllis "Sweetie" Hess, ? Dennison, J. Preshaw, and Florence Madigan. (Courtesy of Chuck Stucker.)

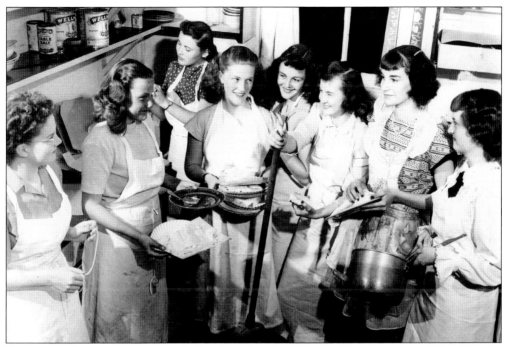

There were also many teenagers who lived on the island. Pictured here are some of the girls who cooked for Warden Johnston's retirement dinner. (Courtesy of Chuck Stucker.)

Just Us Girls was one of the teenage clubs that formed on the island. Here are some of the members around 1940. From left to right are (first row) Katherine Boyd and Joyce Rose; (second row) Betty Waller, Maybeth McKean, and Phyllis "Tiny" Davis; (third row) Ursula Steere and unidentified. (Courtesy of Chuck Stucker.)

Many of the children on the island participated in plays and other performances to entertain family members and guests. Here, three girls perform a dance routine. From left to right are Agnes Roberts, Karen Kirkpatrick, and Betty Ore. (Courtesy of Chuck Stucker.)

Here are the teenagers of the island in 1940. From left to right are (first row) Delmar Tucker, Joyce Rose, and Bob Rebholtz; (second row), Alleene Boyd, Betty Wallar, Kathryn Boyd, and Henry Weinhold; (third row), Bud Stewart, Betty Weinhold, Ursula Steere, Phyllis "Tiny" Davis, Helen Stewart, and Beverly Strucker; (fourth row), George Steere, Dick Stewart, Herb Faulk, Larry Boyd, and unidentified. (Courtesy of Chuck Stucker.)

Charlie Ping, pictured above at a recital around 1937, was one of the first children on Alcatraz. He said 73 years later, "we moved on the island in 1934, almost two months before the first inmates arrived, and lived there for four years. My father was on the hospital staff." His father, C.J. "Cloudy" Ping, worked under Dr. George Hess in the medical ward. After leaving the island, Charlie earned his doctor of philosophy degree from Duke University and became the 18th president of Ohio University, which created the Dr. Charles J. Ping Institute for Teaching the Humanities in his honor. Pictured at right is Cloudy Ping around 1934. (Both, courtesy of Chuck Stucker.)

A childhood friend of Charlie Ping was Roy "Rocky" Chandler. Son of guard E.F. Chandler, Rocky spent four years on the island. Since then, he has published over 60 books, including one on Alcatraz titled *Alcatraz: The Hardest Years, 1934–1938*. Seen here on Easter Sunday 1937 are, from left to right, Clifton "Buster" Mickelson, George ?, Dick ?, Katherine Boyd, Rocky Chandler, Ralph Preshaw, and Heath David. (Courtesy of Chuck Stucker.)

Guys of all ages played football on the island. Chuck Stucker later reflected on the football games: "I remember using black and white footballs for night games so we could see the ball with what light we had." From left to right are Stanley McKean, Jack Fisher, Joe Burdett Jr., Bill Dolby, Ed Faulk, Tom Severson, Chuck Stucker, Dick Martin, Bill Hart, and Jerry Ward. (Courtesy of Chuck Stucker.)

Aside from all the fun they had on the island, the kids still had to go to school every day. This photograph, which appeared in *Collier's* magazine in 1954, shows kids on the boat ride to school. From the San Francisco docks, they were bused to various schools. Most went to public schools in San Francisco, such as Winfield Scott Elementary, Marina Junior High, and Galileo High School. Others attended private schools such as St. Bridges. (Courtesy of Chuck Stucker.)

BOAT SCHEDULE
EFFECTIVE OCTOBER 11, 1959
Leaving Alcatraz

Weekly	Saturday	Sunday	Holiday
A.M.	A.M.	A.M.	A.M.
12:10	12:10	12:10	12:10
6:40	7:05	7:05	7:05
7:20	8:10	8:10	8:10
8:10	9:00	9:00	9:00
10:00	10:00	10:00	10:00
	11:00	11:00	11:00
P.M.	P.M.	P.M.	P.M.
12:45	12:45	12:45	12:45
3:20	3:20	3:20	3:20
3:55	4:55	4:55	4:55
4:40	5:40	5:40	5:40
5:10	7:00	7:00	7:00
5:40	8:45	8:45	8:45
7:00	10:00	10:00	10:00
8:45	11:15	11:15	11:15
10:00			
11:15			
(Reverse Side Leaving Ft. Mason)			
USP-AZ—10-8-59—5C—P			

BOAT SCHEDULE
Leaving Ft. Mason

Weekly	Saturday	Sunday	Holiday
A.M.	A.M.	A.M.	A.M.
12:25	12:25	12:25	12:25
6:55	7:20	7:20	7:20
7:35	8:25	8:25	8:25
8:25	9:15	9:15	9:15
10:15	10:15	10:15	10:15
	11:15	11:15	11:15
P.M.	P.M.	P.M.	P.M.
1:00	1:00	1:00	1:00
3:35	3:35	3:35	3:35
4:10			
4:55	5:10	5:10	5:10
5:25			
5:55	5:55	5:55	5:55
7:15	7:15	7:15	7:15
9:00	9:00	9:00	9:00
10:15	10:15	10:15	10:15
11:30	11:30	11:30	11:30
(Reverse Side Leaving Alcatraz)			

These were the boat schedules to and from the island in 1959. Many of the wives would commute to the city each day for work. (Courtesy of Chuck Stucker.)

Celebrating a birthday party are Sharon (left) and Jean Roberts. (Courtesy of Chuck Stucker.)

On holidays, many of the Alcatraz families would get together and celebrate. There was also Halloween when all the kids, and even the parents, would dress up. In a recollection in the Alcatraz alumni newsletter, one person stated, "Halloween parties were held at the social hall and everyone came in costume." Here are kids in costume in 1936. (Courtesy of Chuck Stucker.)

Christmas was special for everyone on Alcatraz. The children would get together and have dances. Sometimes they would carol all the way up the switchback roads of the island from the social hall to the warden's house, where they would be invited in for cookies and hot chocolate. Above, Warden Edwin Swope and his wife pose in their home during Christmas 1954. Below, teenagers pose at a Christmas dance. (Both, courtesy of Chuck Stucker.)

There was also a live-in Santa Claus on Alcatraz. Lighthouse keeper Ed Schneider, who lived on the island from 1931 to 1955, played Santa for the kids every year. Posing with him are, from left to right, Bill Dolby, Tom Severson, and Joe Burdett. (Courtesy of Chuck Stucker.)

Who would have thought it would snow on Alcatraz? But here it is on the roof of the warden's house. It was January 15, 1962, when San Francisco recorded three inches of snowfall. (Courtesy of Chuck Stucker.)

There were also three weddings on Alcatraz during the penitentiary years. The first was on August 4, 1948, when the lighthouse keeper's daughter Phyllis "Tiny" Davis married Ferris Painter. They are pictured here. (Courtesy of Chuck Stucker.)

The only dog ever to live on Alcatraz was Warden Edwin Swope's dog. He was known by the kids as Pat, but in the Swope household, he was Mr. Patrick. (Courtesy of Chuck Stucker.)

Pictured here is a *Collier's* magazine photograph of the kids of the island in 1954. (Courtesy of Chuck Stucker.)

THE ISLE OF ALCATRAZ
(as seen from the outside)

Staunch and alone in the bay,
Like a fortress grim,
Lashed by angry waves,
Which no man can swim,
Stands the Isle of Alcatraz.

Day by day the ships go by,
Passing on they anchor not,
Merely gaze with solemn wonder,
At that forbidden spot,
Lonely Isle of Alcatraz.

Sailing thru the Golden Gate,
Ships from foreign lands,
Glimpse with scorn upon the rock
Where the prison stands,
Unwelcome Isle of Alcatraz.

Little children fear it,
"Bad men live there" they are told,
Old folks shudder at the thought,
Of those prisoners bold,
Grim old Isle of Alcatraz.

Thus it stands in Frisco Bay,
Where the waters cold,
Dash and beat in fury
Against the challenger bold,
Defiant Isle of Alcatraz.

No fame or honor it attains,
No name of high degree,
Thus daily it sees the ships
Pass on into the sea,
Unfamed Isle of Alcatraz.

Esther Faulk

July 30, 1934.

Here are two poems Esther Faulk wrote about the island in 1934. (Both, courtesy of Chuck Stucker.)

THE ISLE OF ALCATRAZ
(as seen by those who live there)

Out in Frisco's bay of beauty
High above the lashing waves,
Like a battleship on duty
Guarding well the Golden Gate
Stands the Isle of Alcatraz.

Sounds of footsteps hurrying homeward
At the close of day,
Happy voices, children's laughter
Echo out across the bay
From the Isle of Alcatraz.

Cozy homes where love abides,
Where ease and comfort welcomes one,
Where a loved one homeward strides
When his day at work is done,
Welcome Isle of Alcatraz.

The passing ships will never know
The beauty of its cliffs,
Where poppies and sweet flowers grow,
Where beauty lies in secret spots,
Beautiful Isle of Alcatraz.

It cares not for praise or fame,
From the world without,
It cares only to attain
Praise from those within,
Peaceful Isle of Alcatraz.

Ships may come and pass you by,
But you stand in all your glory,
Lift your regal head up high,
We who know you love you,
Our own dear Isle of Alcatraz.

Esther Faulk

July 30, 1934.

Six

OCCUPATION, NATIONAL PARK, AND AMERICAN ICON

1963–2008

The order to close Alcatraz came directly from US attorney general Robert Kennedy on March 23, 1963. Officially, the Federal Bureau of Prisons cited soaring expenses. The costs to run Alcatraz were astronomical, slightly more than $10 a day to sustain each prisoner compared $3 a day at other prisons. The prison facilities were dilapidated, and estimates to refurbish the island ranged from $3 to $5 million. Alcatraz had simply outlived its usefulness. From the island's closure until 1970, following the departure of the lighthouse attendants, Jack and Marie Hart stayed as caretakers.

The island was relatively quiet until November 20, 1969, when a group of Native Americans known as the Indians of All Tribes occupied Alcatraz. This was the longest and largest of three occupations of the island by Native American groups; the first two lasted less than a day. Led by Richard Oakes, the occupation was intended to get the federal government to turn over control of Alcatraz to the Native Americans for a university, museum, and cultural center. Although none of those goals were accomplished, the occupation did lead to other Native American occupations throughout the United States, which eventually resulted in the federal government changing its policy toward Native Americans. As Pres. Richard Nixon put it, "The time has come to break decisively with the past and to create the conditions for a new era in which the Indian future is determined by Indian acts and Indian decisions. Self-determination without termination." The downside of the occupation was vandalism and destruction of the island. A fire destroyed the warden's house and the lighthouse, among other structures. The lighthouse was temporarily disabled, and some 600 pounds of copper wiring was stolen. Federal agents removed the last occupiers on June 10, 1971. In 1972, Congress made Alcatraz part of the Golden Gate National Recreation Area, administered by the National Park Service. Since then, it has become one of the largest tourist attractions in the Bay Area, drawing more than a million people a year.

In addition to being a tourist attraction, Alcatraz also remains a point of interest and controversy. In 2008, San Francisco voters rejected a ballot measure that would have transformed the island into a global center for peace. In 2014, Alcatraz received international attention for hosting Chinese artist and activist Ai Weiwei's exhibit *@Large: Ai Weiwei on Alcatraz* which, according to *Smithsonian* magazine, explored "ideas of confinement and what it means to be a modern political prisoner." In addition to art installations, Alcatraz has been a Hollywood and media sensation since 1962. Alcatraz has become a pop-culture icon, taking hold of America's imagination.

After Alcatraz closed, it was left to the care of Marie and Jack Hart, longtime residents. They cared for the island for seven years, living for one year with the Native American occupiers and leaving in 1970. Here, Jack sits with his boys (from left to right) Bob, Bud, and Bill in the 1950s. (Courtesy of Chuck Stucker.)

All that is left of the Native American occupation led by Richard Oakes is the graffiti. "Indians Welcome" was written above the warning signs on the main dock. The occupation helped to change the relationship between the United States and the Native American tribes forever. (Courtesy of Chantel Elder Photography.)

The most notable damage to Alcatraz during the occupation was from the fire, which destroyed both the warden's and the lighthouse keeper's homes. Above, the fire is seen from a Coast Guard ship on May 30, 1970. At right are the remains of the lighthouse keeper's home and a portion of the warden's house after the fire in 1970. (Above, US Coast Guard. Courtesy of the Golden Gate NRA Park Archives, Office of Resource Management Alcatraz Collection, GOGA 18346.219. Right, US Coast Guard. Courtesy of the Golden Gate NRA Park Archives, Office of Resource Management Alcatraz Collection, GOGA 18346.218.)

It was not until 1972 that a Congressional decree created the Golden Gate National Recreational Area, making Alcatraz a national park. Since then, the island has seen many changes, and most of the residential buildings have been torn down. One of the only residences that still stands is Building No. 64 next to the dock. Alcatraz has also become one of the largest tourist attractions in the national park system. (Courtesy of Chantel Elder Photography.)

Many of the buildings on Alcatraz have been abused by the harsh winds and salt water from the bay. The above photograph shows all that remains of the social hall in 2008; it is left only as a memory to some and a roost for pigeons. Below is the industry building. Once a factory that put hundreds of inmates to work for over 30 years, it is now a silent structure beaten by the bay. (Both, courtesy of Chantel Elder Photography.)

Alcatraz has also been revitalized as a natural habitat for various bird species of the Bay Area. This has created a dilemma for the park service as it tries to accommodate millions of visitors while making sure they do not disrupt the wildlife. The rubble from the old A, B, and C Buildings, along with the associate warden/captain's duplex and the cottages on the parade ground, has found new usage as a habitat for birds. With the help of associations like the Point Reyes Bird Observatory Conservatory Sciences, animals and humans will continue to coexist and flourish on Alcatraz. (Courtesy of Chantel Elder Photography.)

Along with the bird conservatory, Alcatraz has a large agave cactus growth, which covers the south side of the island. Maintained by volunteers, the cactus and the multitude of other plants continue to keep Alcatraz beautiful. (Courtesy of Chantel Elder Photography.)

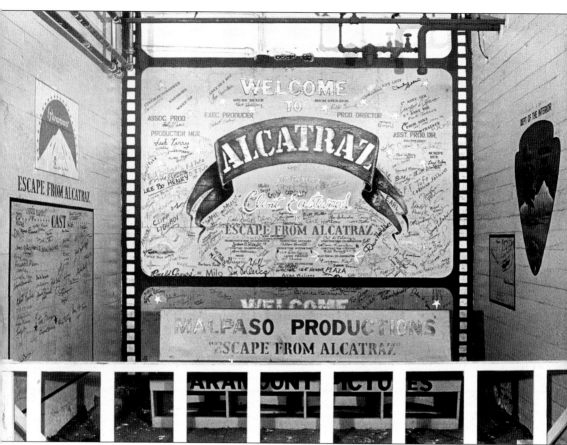

Aside from being one of the most popular tourist attractions in the Bay Area, Alcatraz has also become a huge American pop-culture icon. It has appeared in blockbuster movies, including *Birdman of Alcatraz, Point Break, The Enforcer, Escape from Alcatraz, Murder in the First, The Rock, Catch Me If You Can, X-Men: The Last Stand*, and the *Book of Eli*. In 2012, the science fiction television series *Alcatraz* was produced by J.J. Abrams. It has also appeared in video games such as *Tony Hawk's Pro Skater Four, Tom Clancy's Rainbow Six 3*, and *Call of Duty: Black Ops 2–4* and has been the topic of countless books. The island's legacy as one of America's greatest prisons, as well as the incorrigibles who once inhabited it, keeps it popular among millions. This banner for *Escape from Alcatraz* was signed by members of the cast and crew, including star Clint Eastwood. (Courtesy of the Golden Gate NRA Park Archives, Alcatraz Study Collection, GOGA 18340.)

The memories in the minds of the people who once called the island home—whether prisoners, guards, or family members—live on. The people who shared this unique experience have continually returned to reminisce, share stories, and pass down their histories to the next generation of fans of the island. In this picture, George DeVincenzi returns to where it all began for him. He stands in the prison barbershop, one of his first duty stations. DeVincenzi is one of the narrators on the tour of the cell house heard by millions of visitors every year. He, like many others, is a member of the Alcatraz Alumni Association, a group that tries to preserve the history of Alcatraz through the people who once lived and worked there. (Courtesy of Chuck Stucker.)

Alcatraz continues to remain one of the largest tourist attractions in the San Francisco area. Here are tourists in 2008 exploring the cells of D Block. (Courtesy of Chantel Elder Photography.)

This is the view of the warden's house and the lighthouse from the docks in 2008. (Courtesy of Chantel Elder Photography.)

Alcatraz is shown from the bay in 2008. (Courtesy of Chantel Elder Photography.)

BIBLIOGRAPHY

Armitage, Susan H., Mari Jo Buhle, Danial Czitrom, and John M. Faragher. *Out of Many: A History of the American People.* Upper Saddle River, NJ: Prentice Hall, 2001.

Esslinger, Michael. *Alcatraz: A Definitive History of the Penitentiary Years.* Carmel, CA: Ocean View Publishing, 2003.

Fimrite, Peter. "William Radkay—ex-gangster was favorite at Alcatraz reunions." *San Francisco Chronicle,* September 30, 2006. (www.sfgate.com/cgi-bin/article.cgi?f=/c/a/2006/09/30/BAGK7LFSG31.DTL&hw=alcatraz+radkay&sn=001&sc=1000)

Goodwin, John. *Alcatraz: 1863–1963.* Garden City, NY: Doubleday and Company Inc., 1963.

Larson, Christina. "Why is Ai Weiwei Breaking Into Alcatraz?" *Smithsonian* magazine, October 2014. (www.smithsonianmag.com/arts-culture/why-ai-weiwei-breaking-into-alcatraz-180952742/)

Margolin, Malcolm. *The Ohlone Way: Indian Life in the San Francisco–Monterey Bay Area.* Berkeley, CA: Heyday Books, 1978.

Martini, John A. *Fortress Alcatraz: Guardian of the Golden Gate.* Kailua, HI: Pacific Monograph, 1990.

Stucker, Chuck. *Alcatraz Island History: The Federal Penitentiary Years 1934–1963 from the People Who Lived It.* Dixon, CA: unpublished, 2004.

Discover Thousands of Local History Books Featuring Millions of Vintage Images

Arcadia Publishing, the leading local history publisher in the United States, is committed to making history accessible and meaningful through publishing books that celebrate and preserve the heritage of America's people and places.

Find more books like this at
www.arcadiapublishing.com

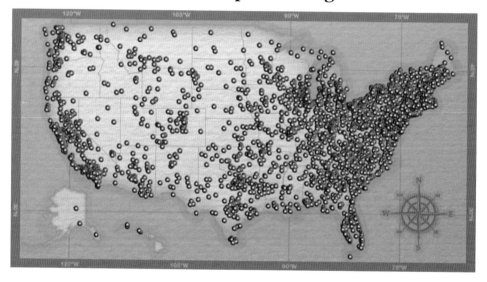

Search for your hometown history, your old stomping grounds, and even your favorite sports team.

Consistent with our mission to preserve history on a local level, this book was printed in South Carolina on American-made paper and manufactured entirely in the United States. Products carrying the accredited Forest Stewardship Council (FSC) label are printed on 100 percent FSC-certified paper.